Get Your Mind Right

Angela J. Walker

Copyright © 2019 Angela J. Walker

All rights reserved.

ISBN: **978-1719527583**

No part of this publication may be reproduced, stored in a retrieval system, or transmitted in any form or by any means-electronic, mechanical, photocopy, recording, or any other, except for brief quotations in printed reviews, without the prior written permission of the author.

Unless otherwise noted, all Scripture quotations are from the King James Version of the Bible.

Scripture quotations marked (AMPC) are from the Amplified Bible. Old Testament @ 1965, 1987 by the Zondervan Corporation. The Amplified New Testament @ 1958, 1987 by the Lockman Foundation

Scripture quotations marked (MSG) are from the Message. Copyright @ 1993, 1995 by Eugene H. Peterson.

Scripture quotations marked (NLT) are from The New Living Translation copyright @ 1996, 2004. Used by permission of Tyndale House Publishers, Inc. Wheaton, Illinois.

Scripture quotations marked (NIV) are from The Holy Bible, New International Version copyright @1973, 1978, 1984. By International Bible Society.

DEDICATION

Giving glory and honor to my Lord and Savior Jesus Christ, who is the head of my life, and who called me for such a time as this. To my husband of 32 years, Pastor Perry Walker, Sr. I love you. You are the love of my youth, my life partner. I thank God for you. To my children, Perry Jr., Charity and Micah, I love each one of you more than anything in this world. You have motivated and inspired me to never give up, to press on and to succeed. You all are my legacy in the earth. I am honored to be your mother. Thank you for always loving and believing in me. To ALL those who have stood with me and believed in the call of God over my life, my faithful friends and loving church family (Deliverance Family Worship Center). I honor you all. To my sisters Linda Allen and Shirley Nathan (Stafford, VA), you both have watched out for me and loved me all my life. You both have been like mothers to me. I am so thankful for the unfailing love and continued support you have always given me. You are amazing big sisters. There is nothing more precious than having people to believe in the call of God in your life. I want to especially honor and thank my Spiritual Parents, Pastors Michael and Kennetha Moore (Faith Chapel/Birmingham, AL). Thank you for holding my hand and walking me through the most difficult season of my life. A special thank you to Reverend Carl and Minister Helen Johnson who have pastored and mentored me continually over the last 30 years. Helen, thank you for helping me with my book. Bishop Silas & Pastor Jennifer Johnson, Pastor Natalie Earl and Pastor Marietha Timmerman. Thank you for your unwavering support, wisdom, love and prayers. Thank you all for helping me to Get and Keep my Mind Right.

CONTENTS

1	What Is A Right Mind	6
2	I Refuse To Die!	11
3	Oh' No, You didn't Act Like that	18
4	Don't Tear Down Your Own House	24
5	Going Through Hell and High Water!	30
6	Stop Worrying About Them	36
7	Letting Go of the Past	40
8	Drop Your Stones	46
9	I Can Do It!	52
10	Living from the Inside Out	57
11	You Have To Love You	61
12	Reclaiming My Time	66

FOREWORD

When I first began to write this book, it was during the most difficult season of my life. It was during that time, that I gained a life changing revelation, of what was necessary, in order for me to not just survive my situation, but to thrive in the midst of it. During my darkest hours, I could hear the Holy Spirit within me admonishing me to "Stay Focused". I could hear the words "Get Your Mind Right", whenever I began to think ungodly thoughts, speak my emotions or doubt the Word of God. These words ignited the purpose and call of God within me. They encouraged and redirected me. They reset my mental processes, my spiritual thermostat and caused me to evaluate what I was thinking about. It was at that time that I was inspired by God and I knew I had to write this book, in order to share with others the importance of getting and keeping their minds right. If you are reading this book you have begun the most important process of your life, which is thought renewal and mind transformation. The light bulb has come on, so to speak, and you have become aware that your thinking needs to be tweaked, changed, or modified in some way. You have taken the first step toward *Getting Your Mind Right* which is acknowledging that there is a need for renewal; therefore, I applaud you! My prayer is that as you read this book that you are transformed by the renewing of your mind by the Word of God. Blessings!

1   WHAT IS A RIGHT MIND?

Proverbs 14:12 KJV "There is a way which seemeth right unto a man, but the end thereof are the ways of death."

Get Your Mind Right!! What exactly do you hear me saying when you hear that statement and what does that statement mean to you? I pray that it is not offensive because it is not meant to offend, but instead it is meant to inspire and motivate. My heart's desire is that every time you read or hear this statement that it will automatically cause you to stop what you are doing and immediately begin to examine your own pattern of thought to determine if your thinking concerning whatever you are dealing with is stemming from a right mind or what is considered a good place. You must remember that just because it seems right to you, does not make it right. How many times in the past, have you thought a certain way about a situation or made an emotionally based decision, later to find out that you were completely wrong in your assumptions and therefore had made your decision in error. What does a right mind look like? How does it process information? How does it respond in a time of crisis? A long time ago I heard the statement that 'mental toughness, mental stability and spiritual maturity' can only be properly evaluated in times of crisis. At that time, I didn't understand the statement, but now I wholeheartedly agree. What they were saying is that when everything is great, we all look strong, we act stable, we function at our optimal potential. Therefore, we truly appear to and believe that we have it all together. But it's in the midst of the crisis, trial and or tribulation that our thought life is truly manifested. It will either save us from turmoil or usher us into utter chaos and despair. Let's define a "right mind". *A right mind consistently functions at a satisfactory level of emotional and behavioral adjustment. It is stable regardless of the situation.* Most of us know when our thinking is off. We know when our thoughts and feelings are not correct or stable. In other words, within ourselves there are times when we are the first to recognize that a situation has us tripping or we know that we are all messed up mentally. We know that something is just not quite right because our spirit is not in agreement with our thoughts and feelings.

Philippians 2:5 KJV "Let this mind be in you, which was also in Christ Jesus:"

What do you think about and how do you respond verbally and behaviorally when you are frustrated, angry, sad or thrust into a crisis situation? Do you give yourself permission to speak and act in a manner that you would not normally do if you were not being driven by your emotions? We identify these times in our life as our mind not being right. We identify our mind as not being right when we find ourselves in situations in which we are unable to control our thoughts and actions. We can't focus on the things that we desire to focus on because our thought life has been invaded by whatever the situation is that is upsetting us. It is at these times, that we feel as though intrusive thoughts are influencing our actions, instead of us feeling as though we are in control. We feel that our thoughts are controlling us and directing our actions. It's at these times that we are forced to acknowledge that we are feeling out of control and it is at this time that we have become aware that our mind is not right. We all have thoughts that are off sometimes, that is not an issue. The issue is when these thoughts become constant and intrusive to the point that you cannot think about anything else and your thought-life is negatively affecting your emotions and actions. It is then that it is time to get your mind right.

Proverbs 19:21 AMPC "Many plans are in a man's mind, but it is the Lord's purpose for him that will stand."

You must take authority over your thought life. All actions are preceded by thoughts. If you want to have a positive outcome, you must have positive thoughts. You must stop, rethink and reframe your negative situation. It is impossible to keep birds from flying over your head or even dropping a surprise from the sky on you occasionally; however, you can keep the birds from building a nest on top of your head. Merely having negative or unhealthy thoughts occasionally is not a major issue within itself. No one can completely control their thoughts. However, you cannot allow your thought life to go unchecked or unchallenged, because eventually what you are thinking will influence your emotions and actions. You must keep it moving. Keep your thoughts moving. Don't become stagnant in your negative thinking. Once you identify a thought as not being what you want to think about, because you have measured it against the standard of what God has established for you to think on, it then becomes your responsibility to stop meditating on it, and to get rid of it by casting it down.

2 Corinthians 10:5 KJV "Casting down imaginations, and every high thing that exalteth itself against the

knowledge of God, and bringing into captivity every thought to the obedience of Christ;"

No one else can do this for you because no one else is inside of your head and privy to what you are thinking. You can look all "put together" on the outside, appear cool and calm, have a smile on your face and, at the same time, be in utter despair and chaos on the inside. This is not the will of God for you. It is my belief that it is impossible to be an unbeliever and be in your right mind; therefore, I am making this statement to believers because I believe, according to scripture, it is impossible to have a "right mind" outside of Christ. A "right mind" is more than just being sane or intellectually competent; having a "right mind" is being profoundly aware of your own insufficiency without Christ's leading and directing you.

Philippians 4:8 KJV "Finally, brethren, whatsoever things are true, whatsoever things are honest, whatsoever things are just, whatsoever things are pure, whatsoever things are lovely, whatsoever things are of good report; if there be any virtue, and if there be any praise, think on these things."

Having a "right mind" is realizing that your way of thinking is twisted, perverted and all together flawed without the continual influence and guidance of the Word of God or the direction of his Spirit within you. A right mind is recognizing your need for a higher power called Jesus Christ. A right mind is knowing that you cannot navigate successfully through this life without Christ. A right mind is knowing that 'true stability' can only be found in Him and that through Him we lack nothing, and we are ready and prepared for everything. Our minds are made right through meditation on the Word of God and by having the standard of our thinking being established by what the Word of God has established for us. Let me give you the key to getting and maintaining a right mind:

Isaiah 26:3 AMPC "You will guard him and keep him in perfect and constant peace whose mind [both its inclination and its character] is stayed on You, because he commits himself to You, leans on You, and hopes confidently in You."

You do not have to carry the weight and responsibility on your own shoulders of getting or keeping your mind right. Your responsibility is to simply read, hear, receive and meditate on the Word of God. It is His responsibility to keep your mind at peace. Wow! That is awesome! God desires to make an exchange. I am a living witness, if you will commit yourself to him, lean on him and hope in him, he will get and keep your mind right!

2   "I REFUSE TO DIE!"

Psalms 118:17 KJV "I shall not die, but live, and declare the works of the Lord"

Have you ever been in so much emotional pain that it felt like the pain itself was going to kill you? I have. I experienced an unimaginable situation that propelled me into the midst of the greatest spiritual battle that I have ever experienced. It was during this experience that I first heard "Get your mind right. This will not kill you!" These are the words that the Holy Spirit spoke to me at the lowest point in my life. I was experiencing my darkest hour. I felt so defeated; I felt like I was in the process of dying emotionally. I cannot adequately find the words to express exactly how excruciating it all was for me at the time. I was in constant emotional pain for almost a full year. I found that merely living was difficult. I literally had to take life one day at a time. I felt so overwhelmed. There were so many challenges during this time in every single area of my life. I was in the midst of severe marital problems, financial challenges, family issues and as a result of all the stress in my life, I had begun experiencing physical issues within my body. It soon became obvious that I was in the midst of a full-blown satanic attack targeting what I loved more than anything in life; my family and ministry. In fact, it was nothing short of a bombardment of satanic proportion. Yet, during it all, I was fully persuaded that I had received a Word from God, instructing me to hold my course. I was also convinced, with everything within me, that the only thing that would sustain me was my faith in this Word. I was determined to hold on to this Word, because I was confident, it would bring me out victoriously. The Holy Spirit had instructed me, to remember and hold on to these words for dear life. I want to encourage you in the same way I was encouraged. I am prophesying to you. You shall also live and not die. Yes, there will be times when it literally feels like what you have or are experiencing is stronger and mightier than your ability to survive it, but hear me, when I tell you *It is not*! During my darkest, most difficult season I often found myself prostrate on the floor in my home. I literally couldn't hold myself upright many times due to my crying and uncontrollable shaking. I constantly cried out to God in frustration, agony and utter despair over the situation that I found myself in.

Proverbs 18:10 AMP *"The name of the Lord is a strong tower; The righteous runs to it and is safe and set on high [far above evil]."*

I must admit that I was very angry. I was angry at everyone, everything and especially myself. I felt as though I was dying a slow death. I realized the pain alone was powerful enough to take me out if I allowed it to. I realized that I had to release this pain in order to stand. I had to take all of the anger I felt and redirect it away from the situation and especially away from myself. I made the conscious decision to place ALL of my feelings of rejection, pain, anger, bitterness and shame back on Satan. I recalled all the many times in my life that I had experienced satanic attacks, they had literally been present all of my life. The purpose of satanic attacks is to stop you from trusting and believing in God. The attacks are to cause you to "cast away your confidence" in the one true God.

Hebrews 10:35-36 AMP *"Do not, therefore, fling away your [fearless] confidence, for it has a glorious and great reward. For you have need of patient endurance [to bear up under difficult circumstances without compromising], so that when you have carried out the will of God, you may receive and enjoy to the full what is promised."*

I decided during the most devastating period in my life, a time when I felt like I was going to lose my mind that I was going to let go and let God have control. I realized during this time that the key to my surviving was my keeping my mind stayed on the Word. Each time that Satan would attack me I would begin to decree out of my mouth that I was going to live and not die and not only that, it is during this season that I decided that I was going to do more than survive my situation. I made up my mind that I was going to use what was devised to destroy me, to instead propel me into my purpose and destiny in life. I became determined to live an abundant and successful life. I made a life changing decision during this time. I decided to stand firmly on the Word of God. What exactly does it mean to stand on the Word? This means that I constantly meditated on and listened to the Word of God. My situation had knocked the breath out of me. It was difficult for me to think clearly at this time. I found simply reading and focusing on the Word of God virtually impossible to do, because of the attack I was enduring. God is so faithful and gracious to me. My spiritual father Pastor Michael Moore was sent by God to minister to my family and I during that season. He personally delivered to our home a full tote and box of CDs for me to listen to. He said "Angela, the Word of God is the answer. It's the only thing that will bring you through what you are going through". I received and grasped a hold of his words. I constantly listened to and meditated on those CDs. I kept my cd player with headphones next to my bed, so that when I went to bed at night or awoke from sleep in the middle of the night, I would listen to the Word. I became totally dependent on the Word, it calmed my spirit. It transformed my thinking. It changed my mindset. It restored the life back to me that my situation had sifted away. Meditating on the Word of God got my mind right. To stand on the Word means you make the Word of God your foundation and source of strength. As a result of constantly standing on the Word, I became stronger and more stable emotionally than I had ever been before. I became confident I was going to live. During this time, I also became keenly aware of the negative impact, all of the stress that I had been experiencing during this period was having on my body. This realization also prompted me to make the life altering decision that I was going to start taking better care of myself than I ever had before. This was very difficult to do at the time. My self-esteem had taken a beaten. I was feeling rejected and worthless. I felt unlovable. Each time I looked in the mirror at myself, I didn't like what I was seeing. I knew that in order to live a victorious life and not look like what I was going through, I had to take care of myself. I had to give to myself what I wanted so desperately to receive from others. Most importantly, I had to focus all my attention on the Word that I had received from the Holy Spirit. I know that His plans for me are that I would not just exist but live a satisfied life. A satisfied life is a well-rounded life that is healthy and complete in every area. It's walking in wholeness, lacking nothing, being content and pleased with my life. To me this meant that I had to become determined to enjoy my family more, travel more and spend more time with friends. Mainly, it inspired me to trust God more, to trust his integrity and his character. He told me more than just that I would not die. He said, "You shall live!". Those words came alive to me. "I shall live and declare the goodness of the Lord." Yes, He is Good! You go through, I go through. But 'through' implies that on the other side is the remainder of the journey.

Psalms 91:16 KJV "With long life will I satisfy him, and shew him my salvation"

On the other side lies what Satan has been trying to keep you from ever entering into. Trusting God's Word of life is more than existing through the difficult process, it's thriving and improving in the midst of the journey so that when you get through to the other side you are in a better position spiritually, intellectually, emotionally, physically and financially to take hold and possess the promises of God. He said, "I shall live". That is such a powerful affirmation that when it is personalized, it brings empowerment to the receiver. I decree to you today that you too shall live and not die. I am not asking you to disregard your feelings, to be in denial about their presence, but to make their importance irrelevant in comparison to the Word you have received from God concerning your situation. What I am saying is that when you feel overwhelmed, defeated, depressed or anxious continuously decree out of your mouth that you shall live and not die. In order to make it through this season you are going to need a right now Word. I remember that during this season I lost my appetite and, as a result, I shed a significant amount of extra weight, I determined that I would allow this weight loss to be for my advantage, so I began to eat three healthy meals a day. I ate when I wasn't hungry, I gave my body what it needed to receive to become healthier than I had ever been before. I had a Word from God and I was determined to come out physically healthier and stronger. Within myself I refused to be forever broken and emotionally crippled. I accept, and I cannot deny that Satan has forged and won some attacks in my life, but I know that the battle belongs to the Lord and I will be declared the winner of it in the end. I knew obeying God would eventually cause me to win. You shall live and not die necessitates living the God kind of life. What I have experienced is nothing new under the sun; others have experienced the same thing and they too have survived. I knew that I could and would make it through this unimaginable situation.

1 Corinthians 10:13 KJV "There hath no temptation taken you, but such as is common to man: but God is faithful, who will not suffer you to be tempted above that ye are able; but will with the temptation also make a way to escape, that ye may be able to bear it."

God always provides a way of escape for the believer. Simply put, God is the way out. Trusting in his Word, in the integrity of His Word during your most difficult times will cause you to prevail. Holding on and believing that God has you is mandatory. Repeating to yourself, "I shall live and not die, I shall live and not die", must be released out of your mouth into the atmosphere. You must know that the turmoil you are currently experiencing is not God's will or plan for your life.

Jeremiah 29:11 AMP "For I know the plans and thoughts that I have for you,' says the Lord, 'plans for peace and well-being and not for disaster, to give you a future and a hope."

During this season you are experiencing a 'firing'. In the pottery making process, before the clay is transformed into the final product it must be processed by fire. Firing converts ceramic work from weak clay into a strong, durable, crystalline glasslike form. This is exactly what will happen to you if you will allow God to use this terrible situation that he did not cause, but yet he will use it to transform your thinking, get your mind right and forever change the trajectory of your life!

James 1:17 KJV *"Every good gift and every perfect gift is from above, and cometh down from the Father of lights, with whom is no variableness, neither shadow of turning."*

Remember, if it is not good, it is not God. No, we don't like tribulation and it is nothing that we would ever just welcome into our lives; however, once we make up our minds that in the midst of the tribulation that we are going to succeed and, yes thrive. After we have endured we will come through stronger and more stable than we have ever been before because we will become persuaded that the Lord God Almighty is our strength. This is the 'firing' process. On the other side of what you are going through is a stronger and wiser version of yourself. On the other side is an individual who has a right mind knowing that you have conquered death through your faith in Christ who conquered it for you. I speak life to you. Yes, if you trust God, you shall live and not die. Fast forward, I made it through. I am on the other side now. The pain is only a memory. I am a living testimony that His grace is sufficient, and His mercies are new every morning. I overcame because I decided to get my mind right!

3 "OH' NO, YOU DIDN'T ACT LIKE THAT!"

Proverbs 25:28 AMP "Like a city that is broken down and without walls [leaving it unprotected] Is a man who has no self-control over his spirit [and sets himself up for trouble]."

Looking back over my life I must admit that there were many times that my behavior was unbecoming as a child of God. No, I didn't curse anyone out (use profanity) or "lay hands on anyone suddenly without prayer", although there were a lot of times I thought about it and wanted to. However, when I found myself feeling disrespected, I did in return display a nasty attitude and behavior that was carnal in nature. Hindsight is 20/20. I can tell you some stories of my past, behavior, and when I say past I am referring to quite a few years ago that would make you question my salvation. Yes, I was saved but my mind was not right when it came to understanding the importance of having control over my own emotions and behavior. Even as a Christian, it is sad, but I must admit that I had no issue confronting you if I felt I was being mistreated or disrespected. No, I was never the type of person to initiate a problem, but by the same token I had no issue with resolving one. I am talking about a time in my life when I had not matured spiritually to the place where I realized and understood that I am always solely responsible for my own response and reactions regardless of the precipitating event, circumstance or situation. I hadn't yet grasped that I was always responsible for my actions and reactions. Nobody can make me act a certain way. Looking back, I must confess that I, of course, felt justified. I felt like my behavior was permissible because of the perceived offense. Most certainly, it was always someone else's fault whenever I acted out of character. I mean they made me act like that because it would not have happened if they had not started it. It was a response to the disrespect or mistreatment I felt I had received at the time. Get Your Mind Right. This is the truth, there is no biblical justification for a believer to ever act like a heathen. Selah, stop and think about it!

Proverbs 17:28 AMP *"Even a fool when he holds his peace is considered wise; when he closes his lips he is esteemed a man of understanding."*

Wow! It's amazing how our actions and reactions are established by what we view as acceptable and unacceptable behavior. If we allow ourselves, we have the ability to justify the craziest of behaviors. Believe me, I have been there, and I understand how sometimes it feels as though you are being picked on, or being targeted with disrespectful behavior from others which causes you to feel as though you are being intentionally enticed or provoked into acting unbecoming. Regardless, YOU are always responsible for your actions and your reactions irrespective of the situation. The individual who is provoking you will have to give an account of their actions the same way that you will have to give an account of your reactions. I don't want to talk about THEM or what THEY have done or did not do. We will address that in another chapter. What I want to deal with right here and now, is your believing that YOU have a "free pass" to act ungodly, just because you feel that you have been pushed, provoked or prodded. Get Your Mind Right. That is carnal reasoning; in other words, that kind of thinking is that of a carnal, immature mind. Your actions and reactions are ALL a reflection of who YOU really are within, just as their actions or reactions are a reflection of who they really are. Your actions and reactions are a mirror reflection of your level of integrity and character. What you do, the words you speak and how you respond, gives the world a glimpse of who you really are within. No! They did not make you do it. I don't care how strongly that you feel they deserved what they got or how you feel they asked for it. You yet remain responsible for your actions in the eyes of God. A child blames others for their behavior and/or their way of thinking. As we mature, we begin to take responsibility for our own actions. YES, there are times when others can see our response or reactions to situations, circumstances or events and they will say that our ungodly behavior is justified. They may even be able to empathize with us by saying that they would have reacted the same way or worst. You must understand that their condoning or cosigning your behavior does not give it legitimacy or make it right. A Right Mind understands that the standard by which it sets itself, is not with that of other, spiritually immature, unrenewed minds. Your "Ride and Die" needs to be exchanged for a "Ride and Live" kind of rider. A Right Mind understands the best and only standard for believers is set by our Lord and Savior Jesus Christ.

Romans 12:2 AMP *"And do not be conformed to this world [any longer with its superficial values and customs], but be transformed and progressively changed [as you mature spiritually] by the renewing of your mind [focusing on godly values and ethical attitudes}, so that you may prove [for yourselves] what the will of God is, that which is good and acceptable and perfect [in His plan and purpose for you]"*

In other words, what would Jesus do? He was tempted just as we are tempted, yet he sinned not. They spit on him. Wow, for most of us, just the thought of someone spitting on us causes us to feel indignation, to the point that we automatically give ourselves permission to act inappropriately. Jesus was spat on and He did not retaliate. He is our example. You may be thinking, I am not Jesus. No, you are not, however, you are a Christian, therefore you are called to be like him. He is our example. When I was spiritually immature, I felt justified in "going off" on people whom I felt deserved to be gone off on! I had no tolerance for what I deemed as intentional, disrespectful behavior toward me, and as a result, I gave myself permission to act ungodly. Think of it this way, going off on people for whatever reason is a demonstration of lack of self-control on your part. Scripture states, that individual is like a vulnerable city. This means that your out of control behavior opens you up for attack by the enemy. Your lack of control has removed your spiritual defenses. How is that possible? When we act ungodly we remove ourselves from under the umbrella of God's guidance and protection. We are not receptive to God's influence when we lose control. As I have matured I now realize that how I react is never about the other individual, but that it is always about me and where my mind is at that particular time.

Matthew 15:11 NLT "It's not what goes into your mouth that defiles you; you are defiled by the words that come out of your mouth."

The best example I can think of is the *jostling* of a cup. What happens when you jostle a full cup? The answer to that is simple. Its contents will overflow or spill out of the cup. Likewise, when you are provoked the only thing that can flow out of you is what you contain within your heart and mind. Jostling does not put anything into you; that is why it is not the other individual's actions that caused you to act like you acted or say what you said. When you behave improperly, it is because acting improperly was within you. Jostling simply releases or manifests the contents of the heart. The jostling did NOT put profanity into you. Jostling did not make you SNAP or speak in a way that you would later regret speaking. Jostling does not put anything into the cup, no more than your being mistreated or wronged put your retaliatory behavior into you. Outside issues do not penetrate into the cup. Only what the cup possesses can spill out or be released during times of provocation or tribulation. It is impossible for anything to come out of you that does not reside within you. I am trying to help you. The truth that you receive shall make you free. Get Your Mind Right!

Luke 6:45 AMP "The upright (honorable, intrinsically good) man out of the good treasure [stored] in his heart produces what is upright (honorable and intrinsically good), and the evil man out of the evil storehouse brings forth that which is depraved (wicked and intrinsically evil); for out of the abundance (overflow) of the heart his mouth speaks"

Difficulty, stress, and crisis tend to cause an outpouring of what is hidden in our inner being. Things slip out that sometimes we ourselves were unaware that we possessed within. They may have been hidden deep within our subconscious. Perhaps we had not experienced that level of anger or hurt in such a long time or ever so that we never had to draw that deep within for a reaction or response. A Right Mind takes responsibility for its' actions and uses life experiences to grow. I have acted a fool too in the past, but now MY mind is Right, and I declare I will never be found in that place again. I used to think that to allow people to talk to me any kind of way or treat me disrespectfully was a sign of weakness in me. NO, on the contrary, I now realize that how someone treats me says nothing about me, but instead, how an individual treats others is a reflection of who they are within. An individual's actions and reactions are a reflection of their individual character and spiritual maturity. Lack of self-restraint in what you say and do, is a characteristic of a spiritually weak individual.

Proverbs 16:32 AMP *"He who is slow to anger is better than the mighty, he who rules his [own] spirit than he who takes a city".*

I decree that you are allowing the Holy Spirit to do a work in you. I am now thankful for whatever experiences that I have had that allowed me to develop and grow. No, I am not glad that I've gone through the bad experiences that I have gone through, but I am profoundly thankful for the good that has resulted as a result of those experiences. Strive to be able to say that because of what you have experienced that you are better, stronger, wiser and more spiritually minded.

4   DON'T TEAR DOWN YOUR OWN HOUSE!

Proverbs 14:1 AMP "Every wise woman builds her house: but the foolish one tears it down with her own hands"

You would think an individual insane if you heard of or if you were witnessing them demolishing their own home. Your mind could not fathom something so absurd. Why? Because you would say that there is no plausible reason or logical explanation to justify an individual tearing down something that belongs to them. An individual's home should always be viewed as precious and irreplaceable to them. We would only expect that individual to be the defender and protector of their home and property. We would expect for their home to mean more to them than anyone else in the world. No one should appreciate the value of a home more than its occupants or owners. Watching the deterioration or demolishment of a home in most instances is always a sad occasion, especially if when we look at the home, we can imagine that with a little vision and some hard work that the home is still salvageable and can be restored. The home is symbolic and represents the family. When I talk about the home I am not just talking about the physical building or structure. I am talking about the family that the home represents. The home is the dwelling place of the family. As the dwelling place of the family it is full of memories, mementos and keepsakes. The home symbolizes the life and accomplishments of the family. When it is torn down or destroyed it is a visible expression of the lack of care, commitment and vision that it has received. Likewise, when our nuclear family unit is torn down or destroyed, it too can be traced back to a lack of care, commitment and vision. Unknowingly, this is exactly what happens more often than not, when we become frustrated, angry, sad or disappointed. We engage in behavior that is ultimately self-destructive and therefore destructive to all those connected to us. We have become the bull in the china shop, except for the china shop is our homes. Let go of the hurt, not for the one who hurt or wronged you, but so that you are no longer perpetuating the hurt, pain and destruction in your own life, family and relationships.

Ephesians 4:31-32 AMPC "Let all bitterness and wrath and anger and clamor [perpetual animosity, resentment, strife, fault-finding] and slander be put away from you, along with every kind of malice [all spitefulness, verbal abuse, malevolence]. Be kind and helpful to one another, tender-hearted [compassionate, understanding], forgiving one another [readily and freely], just as God in Christ also forgave [a]you."

There is no greater damage that can be done to a home than the damage that can be inflicted by the occupants of that home, because that individual knows all the faults and weaknesses of the home. They know exactly where to attack to cause the greatest damage; they know what will cause its quickest demise. They know exactly what will ultimately weaken it beyond repair. They know where the attack will be most effective. What we don't realize is that the individual that tears down their own house is cutting off their own nose to spite their face. They may be in so much pain that they can't see straight, and this is exactly what Satan wants to happen. Get Your Mind Right!!! You are destroying your own home!!! I know that this is not your intent. I know that this is the last thing that you wanted to happen. But, regardless, in the spiritual realm this is exactly what is happening. Every time that you lose spiritual and emotional control, and you open your mouth and begin to speak your emotions; cursing, yelling or ranting, YOU are actively tearing down YOUR own home because, in reality your behavior is destructive. It is impossible to behave carnally and reap spiritually. Your actions are not beneficial in any way. Your actions are now causing further damage to your family.

Galatians 6:8 AMPC "For the one who sows to his flesh [his sinful capacity, his worldliness, his disgraceful impulses] will reap from the flesh ruin and destruction, but the one who sows to the Spirit will from the Spirit reap eternal life."

Losing control of our fleshly emotions is always a negative thing and it always carries with it negative consequences. We are out of order every time that we open our mouth for the purpose of inflicting emotional pain on someone else. If our intent when we speak, is to enact revenge, or to cause the other individual, to feel shame, embarrassment, anger or to cause the person, to feel or experience the pain we are feeling, then our motive is completely wrong. Speaking our emotions is a demonstration of our lack of self-control and is always a sign of spiritual weakness. Satan wants us to harbor and allow our pain and anger to take control of our lives, to the point that we don't even realize that we are out of control. He knows that when this happens, we have become reckless, and we are on a rampage causing destruction everywhere that we go. Perhaps you may not have realized that you have been out of control in times past or even up until now with not just your words but with your actions. There is never any acceptable explanation for you to become verbally assaultive or even worst for you to put your hands on another individual. When it gets to that point, you are completely in the wrong and you are not in your right mind. There is simply no excuse for your behavior, and no one wants to be around an angry, bitter, out of control individual.

Proverbs 21:19 KJV "It is better to dwell in the wilderness, than with a contentious and an angry woman."

I don't care what he or she did or did not do. You do not have permission to curse them out, slander their name, burst their windows, cut their tires or destroy their property. You do not have permission or justification to walk in anger, bitterness and unforgiveness. Whenever you allow or condone ungodly behavior in yourself or others as being acceptable behavior, as a result of an offense, regardless of whether you know it or not, you are wrong. Entertaining as acceptable these kinds of thoughts or behavior is a result of not having a right mind. You are now in the process of tearing down your own home every time you begin to act on or meditate on ungodly thoughts and behavior. I understand that you were hurt. I understand that your actions may simply be a reaction or response to the turmoil you are experiencing inwardly, as a result of an offense committed against you. Nevertheless, in the midst of the hurt, you cannot lose sight of your responsibility to respond or react appropriately. Two wrongs do not make a right. You are still responsible for your actions and if your response is retaliatory, then you are still wrong! That's right, I am speaking to you right now and I want to tell you that you are wrong, and you are tearing down your own home. I want to get your attention. I know that this is not the real you. You are hurting. You are not at yourself, because I know that you would not intentional do what is being done. You are mismanaging your pain and your anger. We have heard the statement that "hurting people hurt people".

Well, I want to say that hurting people first hurt themselves and then they hurt other people. It is NOT too late to change. Perhaps you are thinking that it is too late to undo what you have done, it may be. I honestly don't know. But, I do know that it is not too late to start from where you are at this very moment and begin engaging the rebuilding process. Remember, you are only responsible for your actions and you can only do what you can do. Having a right mind is the best place to start.

Job 22:28-30 AMPC "You shall also decide and decree a thing, and it shall be established for you; and the light [of God's favor] shall shine upon your ways. When they make [you] low, you will say, [There is] a lifting up; and the humble person He lifts up and saves. He will even deliver the one [for whom you intercede] who is not innocent; yes, he will be delivered through the cleanness of your hands."

You have the ability by your words and actions to build up your home and family the same way that you were able to tear it down. Okay, perhaps you are not the one who tore it down, you can still choose to be the initiator of the rebuilding process. What are you saying about your home and family? What do you see in your future? Always remember that you are responsible for the upkeep of your own home. How many times have you admired how someone else's yard or home looked. Their grass may be perfectly edged or mowed as you simultaneously observed that your property was in desperate need of a manicure or attending to. The reason that someone else's family and home is in good condition is because someone is taking care of it. Satan is after ALL our families. He is not a respecter of persons. Even though it feels like your family was singled out for an attack. You are not the first and you will not be the last. Listen to me, hear me loud and clear, no stranger off of the streets is going to come take care of what belongs to you unless they are coveting it for themselves. Stop waiting for someone else to come to your rescue, to fix your family and home for you. It's yours, you need to assume all the rights and responsibilities of lawful ownership. Make up your mind that you are going to be the one that stand in the gap for your family, regardless of what someone else does or does not do. They need you to get your mind right so that you can fight for them. It is time to stop tearing down your own house with your words and actions and to Get Your Mind Right!

5   GOING THROUGH HELL & HIGH WATERS

Isaiah 43:2 AMP "When thou passest through the water, I will be with thee; and through the rivers, they shall not overflow thee. When thou walkest through the fire, thou shalt not be burned, neither shall the flame kindle upon thee"

It is impossible to journey through this earthly life without eventually encountering a season when you feel that you are walking through the valley of the shadow of death or through waters that are completely over your head. Perhaps you have already experienced times in your life when you felt you were in the midst of despair, a period of time when you felt completely overwhelmed, depressed or even suicidal. At times like this, you may feel utterly defeated. During these times, it does not matter what brought you to this point. Pointing the finger will not fix your problem. It does not matter if it was due to physical or emotional neglect or abuse, whether it was due to family or marital problems, financial lack, prolonged or chronic illness. It doesn't matter if you ended up in the valley as a consequence of your own actions or if it was another individual's actions that placed you there. All that matters at that particular moment is surviving and getting through that very difficult time. I am convinced that mindset is everything! It is during these times that you will realize that your belief system or your mindset is the predominate thing that is going to make the difference between whether you walk in victory or succumb in defeat. There will be times that you will feel completely and totally overwhelmed and ill prepared to navigate through the circumstances, situations or events that you have been thrusted into.

Psalm 3:4 KJV "I cried unto the Lord with my voice, and he heard me out of his holy hill. Selah"

There will be times when you will struggle to maintain your confession of faith, times when you will *feel* totally alone and abandoned by God, family and friends. Times when you feel that no one could possibly understand the depths of depression, pain, anxiety or despair that you are going through, times when your personal struggle has made you feel that totally isolating yourself both emotionally and physically from the entire world is the only way you can protect yourself from further pain, harm and disappointment. During these times the actions that you have taken to protect yourself result only in your having intensified those feelings and reinforced your belief that you are walking through your particular experience alone and that no one can help you in any way. Being attacked with feelings of loneliness is just a small piece of the puzzle. There will be times when you will feel so ashamed of where you have found yourself in every way. Ashamed of not feeling confident, ashamed of not feeling strong, ashamed of feeling weak, feeling inadequate or like you are not enough. You feel ashamed of being afraid, ashamed of being who you feel you have become. While in the valley I found myself both afraid to live and afraid to die. I was afraid to live because the present pain was excruciating, and I didn't know how much more I could handle without breaking. I was constantly wondering how much longer would I have to endure in my valley. While in the valley, it seems like death is always present. In a way I believe that the valley is a form of death. A part of you dies, life as usual dies, your dreams die, your hopes die, and all pretense also dies. The valley brings you to the reality of what remains when all pretense has vanished, and everything unanchored has been stripped away. Your old self dies, and you are left with the new you, the you that has survived the valley.

Psalms 124: 6-8 KJV "Blessed be the Lord, who hath not given us as a prey to their teeth. Our soul is escaped as a bird out of the snare of the fowlers: the snare is broken, and we are escaped. Our help is in the name of the Lord, who made heaven and earth"

While in the valley, I was preoccupied with thoughts of loss and death which were caused by the feelings of rejection and betrayal I had experienced. I remember being afraid to die because I knew that I was so unhappy with the culmination of the life I currently had lived. As I looked at my life I was consumed with feelings of disappointment. It all felt like a bad nightmare and I was unwilling to accept that this was my new normal. My experiences had left me feeling sad and dissatisfied with where I was in life. I did not want to die feeling that I had not accomplished my God given purpose in the earth. It is at this time that I realized I was actively in the midst of fighting my biggest battle. It was at this time that I really understood that the battleground was not in my marriage, finances or health. I realized that the battleground was in my mind. It seemed like it would never end. At these times you will probably also experience a disruption in your sleep pattern, because the devil usually attacks the believer in their sleep because he understands that lack of sleep will eventually decrease your ability to think clearly and soberly. Sleep deprivation will eventually also lessen your emotional fortitude and resilience. I believe that it is mentally healthy and spiritually acceptable to acknowledge where you are at during this time.

Acknowledging that you are in the valley is okay, but equally important is knowing that you do not have any intent of staying where you are and that you see yourself as simply passing through.

Psalms 23:4 NLT "Even when I walk through the darkest valley, I will not be afraid, because you are close beside me. Your rod and staff protect and comfort me."

At this time, it is irrelevant what is the cause of you being where you are or who is to be blamed for your being in this particular situation of where you are currently. Lamenting over what you are having to face does not help either, it is not constructive or productive. Getting Your Mind Right is the first order of business in order for you to begin to thrive, not just survive in the valley. Satan is a liar, you are not alone. God is with you!

Psalms 139:8 KJV "If I ascend up into heaven, thou art there: if I make my bed in hell, behold, thou art there."

He is with you continually and He has sent the Holy Spirit to comfort you. You must not forget that you are passing through the 'valley' and that you recognize it is not your final destination. Do not build a permanent dwelling structure in the valley. Do not allow yourself to accept your current situation as permanent or irreversible. Regardless of how it feels at this moment, it is just temporary. Refuse to accept your temporary feelings as your permanent normal. The devil is a liar and the truth is not in him! Don't you stop moving. Keep putting one foot in front of the other. You are walking through your valley even now, just keep doing what you are doing. Keep it moving! A right mind understands that even though the time in the valley seems unending, it has an expiration date and a time limit. While walking through this season, what makes it more doable, and what allows you to go through it and come out of it, not looking like what you have been through, is totally based on your mindsight while in the midst of your difficult season. If you truly believe that you are going to survive your experience and that on the other side of your personal valley is a better, happier place for you, that belief will empower you to keep moving forward. Therefore, don't focus on your valley, focus on your promised land.

2 Cor 4:16-18 AMP "Therefore we do not become discouraged [spiritless, disappointed, or afraid]. Though our outer self is [progressively] wasting away, yet our inner self is being [progressively] renewed day by day. For our momentary, light distress [this passing trouble] is producing for us an eternal weight of glory [a fullness] beyond all measure [surpassing all comparisons, a transcendent splendor and an endless blessedness]! So, we look not at the things which are seen, but at the things which are unseen; for the things which are visible are temporal [just brief and fleeting], but the things which are invisible are everlasting and imperishable"

This belief will also influence the way you take care of yourself and the progress you make while in the valley. True enough, I cannot change certain areas of my life, however I can work on improving others even in difficult times. So much is up to you, if you set your mind on just surviving your ordeal, then that is simply all you will do, but if you set your mind on thriving in the midst of what you are experiencing, then that is what will happen. You are the prophet of your own life. What do you see and what are you speaking about your current situation? Decree out of your mouth "yea though I walk through the valley of the shadow of death,

I will fear no evil, for thou art with me". I am so very proud of you! From personal experience, I know that the valley of despair is a horrible place to be in. It is a place of constant satanic attacks. Being in the valley alone can be a paralyzing place of fear. I want you to just take a quick time out right now and pat yourself on the back for being a survivor. You see, surviving gives God something to work with. Surviving is the first part of both succeeding and being successful. Some who have gone through less than what you have gone through have ended up in psychiatric hospitals due to mental breakdowns, prisons due to exacting revenge or the grave as a result of not feeling they could fight any longer, but you are still here, therefore I applaud you! Don't stop here, let this be your launching pad into the best season of your life. You are getting your mind right and I decree that the best for you is on the other side of the hell and high water.

6   STOP WORRYING ABOUT THEM

Luke 6:28-30 AMP "Bless and show kindness to those who curse you, pray for those who mistreat you. Whoever [a]strikes you on the cheek, offer him the other one also [simply ignore insignificant insults or losses and do not bother to retaliate—maintain your dignity]. Whoever takes away your coat, do not withhold your shirt from him either. Give to everyone who asks of you. [b]Whoever takes away what is yours, do not demand it back."

We are all navigating through our individual life journeys. You can not experience life for anyone else and no one else can experience life in your place. You are doing yourself a tremendous disservice, when you focus all your time and energy, on being obsessed with what other people are thinking or saying about you. So many times, in life, it feels like our problems would decrease or our situation would improve significantly, if others would simply either treat us right or leave us alone. Our lives probably would be less chaotic, if they would stop causing or instigating drama in our lives, behave a certain way or would respond differently. Perhaps, our life would be easier if they would, but our lives can't remain in limbo, while we wait for them to say or do something differently. You never want to take that stance because by doing so, you have just assumed the posture of a victim instead of that of a victor. When you attribute credit to or blame someone else for the condition of your life, you are subsequently relinquishing your power to them. It is faulty thinking to believe that if someone else had not did what they did or if they would only do things differently that your situation or feelings would improve or change. If that is the truth, then your life is not of your own making, but it is up to and under the control of others. No, that is not the truth. That is the lie that Satan wants us to believe, because then it immobilizes us and causes us to always be absorbed and focused on the imaginary power of *them*, instead of focusing on and working to improve ourselves. Focusing on other people is one of the biggest distractions in the lives of believers. As long as your focus is on what other people are thinking, saying or doing, you have not taken ownership of the condition of your life, therefore your mind is not right.

Psalms 25:1-2 KJV "Unto thee, O Lord, do I lift up my soul. O my God, I trust in thee: let me not be ashamed, let not mine enemies' triumph over me."

I want you to take a moment right now, to think about all the time, energy and effort that you have wasted worrying about 'them'. The truth is that we are not in control and we will never have control of what others think, say or do. It is impossible. We will never be able to control 'them'. What they do is not our responsibility or business. That's right, as much as we wish we could control the circumstances, situations and events of our lives, we can't. We will never be able to control other people's thoughts about us, their actions toward us or reactions regarding us. You cannot make anyone else treat you the way you want to be treated. You cannot make them love you, want to be around you, respect you, or value you. Trying to do so will only make you unhappy, bitter, resentful and miserable. You must accept that you are powerless in your ability to govern someone else's actions. However, you can gain strength and peace in knowing that you can control your actions and responses concerning whatever happens in your life. That's right, your journey is not about others, it's not about them. Your life journey has never been and will never be about them. Your life journey is about how you navigate through this world. Your journey is about your interactions with others; specifically, your actions, reactions and the decisions that you make in your life. Your life journey has always been about you discovering your purpose for existing in the earth and learning to fulfill that purpose.

Romans 14:12-14 AMP "So then, each of us will give an account of himself to God. Then let us not criticize one another anymore, but rather determine this— not to put an obstacle or a stumbling block or a source of temptation in another believer's way."

Blaming 'them' continually keeps you distracted and in victim mode. Perhaps subconsciously you are content with being a victim because it does not require any culpability from you for your own actions or current situation. This kind of thinking creates an attitude of complacency and victimization. In reality the only power that other people have in your life is the power that you have willfully relinquished to them. Get Your Mind Right is understanding that their power in your life is limited to the power that you have rendered or assigned to them. Truth be told, they become non-factors the minute you take back the power that you have given to them. Think about it. Who are they anyway? Do 'they' have a hell or heaven to place you in? No, they don't. What can they actually do to you without your permission? What is their actual power or significance in your life?

Isaiah 53:17 KJV "No weapon that is formed against thee shall prosper; and every tongue that shall rise against thee in judgment thou shalt condemn. This is

the heritage of the servants of the Lord, and their righteousness is of me, saith the Lord."

Let's identify who the 'them' are in your life? They are whoever you have made more important and assigned more power to influence your life than the Word of God. You focus more on them than the Word, you talk more about what they are saying, and value their opinion more than you do obeying what God's Word is saying to you. Your 'them' can be as random as the cashier in the local grocery store, a Facebook friend who you have never met, a close friend of the family, family member or spouse. It really doesn't matter who 'them' is. The point is that God wants to have final authority in your life. Understandably, there will be times that you will feel it necessary to receive support from others, and I understand that it feels better to be supported, however there are times in our lives when we may not have the support of anyone else and at those times we must be okay with accomplishing the journey alone. I always like to think of it this way, when we each die, we are going to stand before God alone. We are not going to stand before him with our significant other, our support system or our entourage with us. It is going to be totally about how we navigated through this life, specifically our actions and responses. I may not have control over everything that happens to me, but I have control over my response to my experiences and those responses reflect my individual character and integrity. They or 'them' will no longer control my life and destiny. I have taken my authority back and as a result I am free to live my life liberated from the influence and power of 'them'.

7 LETTING GO OF THE PAST!

Philippians 3:1 KJV "Brethren, I count not myself to have apprehended; but this one thing I do, forgetting those things which are behind, and reaching forth unto those things which are before"

I have been a minister's wife for over 30 years and during this time I have had the privilege of talking and ministering to hundreds of people while they were in the midst of going through terrible life situations. One common denominator that I have observed is that no one is immune to having problems. At one time or another in all of our lives, we will experience some form of tribulation. Although we all experience tribulation, we don't all have the same outcome. I have found that the difference is dependent on our ability to let go of the past and move forward. I have witnessed that those who were willing to regroup and move forward were always the ones who overcame the obstacles that they were facing and went on to experience success. Those individuals and families who were unwilling for whatever reason to let go and move beyond the hurt, pain, offense or disappointment were the ones who seemingly remained stuck and experienced failure. Often in these situations, I would hear the individuals involved state, "I can't forgive" or "I can't let go of it".
 No one is asking you to forget, or even to forgive at this time. I am presenting to you that forgiveness is a decision and not a feeling. Forgiveness happens instantly. Although, I also believe that getting past the

pain and walking in the full manifestation of your complete healing can be a gradual process. Depending on the level of the pain involved and the offended individual's spiritual maturity. For some individuals, full recovery or restoration can be a lengthy process for them. In many instances, true forgiveness is not manifested until later on down the road. There first has to be a willingness to let go of the past and move forward. Letting go consists of being willing to trust God with your past, with the event, circumstance or situation that you have experienced. You have to be willing to surrender the pain, hurt, disappointment, and offense to Him. You must be willing to trust God to vindicate you. To make your being done wrong, right. You have to be at least willing to give God your life or what I would categorize as the remnant or what is left of your life. You have to be willing to let it go. You must believe that God can and will take your ashes and give you beauty, take your shame and give you joy, take your test and turn it into a testimony.

Isaiah 43:18-19 NIV "Forget the former things; do not dwell on the past. See, I am doing a new thing! Now it springs up; do you not perceive it? I am making a way in the wilderness and streams in the wasteland"

Listen to me, you survived the event, circumstance and situation that Satan devised to try to destroy you. Look at the enormity of what you have been through. Satan desired to sift you as wheat. The devil desired to take you out, but you are still here by the grace of God. You may not be who or what you want to be, but you are still here. You made it through what would have caused most people to lose their minds, end up in prison or simply give up on life and die. But not you, you have prevailed as victor. You didn't give up. You may not have done everything perfectly or even came through it the way you had beforehand dreamed or imagined, but nevertheless you came through. Congratulations, I applaud you! I personally know the struggle, the emotional energy, mental wherewithal, the spiritual resiliency that it took for you to make it to where you are now. I have been there. I personally experienced an unimaginable situation, that I too thought was going to destroy my ministry, my family and my life. I could not fathom at the time how we would get through or survive it. But, by the grace of God we did. Therefore, I am speaking to you from experience. I know how you are feeling, because I know how I felt. I know that you may not remember the events of the day to day journey you have experienced. I don't. Trauma has been known to cause time gaps in memory. Sure, you remember the specific details of your particular situation. However, although the facts may be so detrimental or painful that you may never forget. You most likely do not remember the day to day journey of what you have been through, or how you managed to make it to where you are now. You have been through a storm. Now, you will have to face the devastation that has resulted. I want you to realize that you have outlasted and survived the most difficult time of your life. You should be celebrating, and I am honored to celebrate with you.

2 Corinthians 12:9 AMP "but He has said to me, "My grace is sufficient for you [My lovingkindness and My mercy are more than enough—always available—regardless of the situation]; for [My] power is being perfected [and is completed and shows itself most effectively] in [your] weakness." Therefore, I will all the more gladly boast in my weaknesses, so that the power of Christ [may completely enfold me and] may dwell in me."

As a teenager I attended a Pentecostal church occasionally, and as a result, to my advantage, I now dance in the spirit when I really want to praise God. I'm rejoicing with you and dancing about your victory right now. Hear me loud and clear, I am talking to you. It's time to move forward! Looking at the aftermath of your situation may seem enormous; however, it is up to you to have the right mindset and realize that because you survived the storm, that you WILL most definitely survive the cleanup after the storm. How do you do that? You decide to 'move forward'. You may not realize it at this moment, and it may not sound like comforting words to you right now, but I guarantee you that you are stronger now than before you went through what you went through. You are not only stronger, but you are also wiser. You should also be more confident in your resiliency because of what you have been through. I encourage you to allow God to complete the process. In other words, don't allow Satan to use what you experienced and went through as a snare to keep you entangled in regret, self- condemnation and bitterness for the rest of your life. I want to give you permission to forgive yourself. Please, forgive yourself. Let yourself off the hook, let yourself be vulnerable, let yourself be okay with messing up, missing the mark, missing the signs, misinterpreting the situation, reacting inappropriately, speaking the wrong words, the wrong way, at the wrong time. Holding on too long, letting go too soon or perhaps not doing enough. It really doesn't matter at this moment what it is. I'm not judge or jury. I do know that all healing and health involves letting go of the past so that you can move forward to the future. In all honesty, I don't have any authority in your life and I understand that. I just know from personal experience, during my most difficult time, when I was my most devastated. I knew I had to let it go for my own mental health. I wanted and needed someone to tell me that it was okay to let go of the past, forgive myself and move forward. I now understand that forgiveness itself is an indication of both spiritual maturity and mental stability.

Ezekiel 1:12 KJV "And they went everyone straight forward: whither the spirit was to go, they went; and they turned not when they went"

Moving forward is the result of being in a right mind, just as not wanting to move forward indicates that you are not in your right mind. Healing can only begin when you become willing to let go of the pain. Wow, I struggled really hard with letting go. I think subconsciously I felt that the longer I held onto the situation demonstrated how affected I had been by it. Many times, we make holding onto the past our personal memorial to the event. I was tremendously affected by my experience, and how else would those who hurt me, know how greatly I was affected if I quickly let it go and moved forward. I was devastated, I was hurt. At the time I didn't want to appear weak by appearing to minimize it. I spent a long period of time wondering if I was going to lose my mind. It is then that I received the revelation, that holding on to the past was not a demonstration of strength but instead it was a sign of weakness. Being strong was demonstrated in my ability to press beyond the pain and continue my life. I realized that holding on was not working for me, it did not serve my purpose or best interest. It was causing me harm by making my life miserable. It is unhealthy and biblically wrong to 'NOT Forgive', not just others but mainly ourselves. Individuals who have difficulty forgiving others are the very people who also struggle with forgiving themselves. Perhaps you have committed some kind of wrong, offense, sin, betrayal or injury to someone else or maybe you were the individual who experienced hurt or offense. Let's talk about 'moving forward'. I am going to assume that you have asked God to forgive you first of all, and then I am believing that you have asked the individual who you hurt for their forgiveness. There is most likely nothing else that can be done to make amends or remedy the situation. We cannot rewind time; however, we can accept and walk in God's grace. Repent, learn from our experience and move forward. I want to encourage you to release others and to most importantly let yourself off the hook. Let go of the past. Move forward and begin again!

1 John 1:9 AMP "If we [freely] admit that we have sinned and confess our sins, He is faithful and just [true to His own nature and promises], and will forgive our sins and cleanse us continually from all unrighteousness [our wrongdoing, everything not in conformity with His will and purpose]."

8   DROP YOUR STONES!

Matthew 7:1-5 MSG "Don't pick on people, jump on their failures, criticize their faults - unless, of course, you want the same treatment. That critical spirit has a way of boomeranging. It's easy to see a smudge on your neighbor's face and be oblivious to the ugly sneer on your own. Do you have the nerve to say, 'Let me wash your face for you,' when your own face is distorted by contempt? It's this whole traveling roadshow mentality all over again, playing a holier-than-thou part instead of just living your part. Wipe that ugly sneer off your own face, and you might be fit to offer a washcloth to your neighbor"

I am going to be very transparent, of all the chapters of this book, this one on dropping the stones has personally been the hardest chapter for me to write. Even as I am in the process of writing it, I am experiencing the strengthening of the Holy Spirit. It is the truth regardless of if it is what we want to do or not. Walking in forgiveness toward those who have insulted, offended, mistreated or wronged us, is always the will of God. Forgiveness an act of faith and grace that our flesh will always try to resist. Let me just put this out there. I am currently walking through the process of dropping the stones and not picking them back up again also. In the spirit, daily I can yet hear the Holy Spirit, telling me to "drop the stones to the ground, that I have in my hands, for the purpose of attacking and condemning those who hurt me, and to then back away from them slowly", can't you? Forgiveness is a choice. I believe that it happens instantly. However, moving past the pain and anger is a process for most believers. I was severely wounded. I was wronged and as a result, my experience left me feeling like I had a right to hold a grudge, judge and retaliate against my offenders, but I was wrong, I don't! God commands, not asks us to forgive. Forgiveness is not an option for the believer. Unforgiveness separates us from the Father by hindering our prayers from being answered.

Matthew 5:23-24 KJV "Therefore if thou bring thy gift to the altar, and there rememberest that thy brother hath ought against thee; Leave there thy gift before the altar, and go thy way; first be reconciled to thy brother, and then come and offer thy gift"

Dropping the stones is an action that benefits the forgiver more than it does the one that hurt us, and who is being forgiven. Listen to me, anger and unforgiveness only corrode the vessel that possesses it. Holding on to anger and unforgiveness is like drinking poison and expecting the other individual to die. Despite how holier than thou that we can sometimes pretend to be, none of us are righteous within or by our own making. It does not cost us anything worth holding on to, for us to be merciful to others. Grace is unmerited favor. It is being nice, kind and loving towards people when we do not feel that they are deserving or worthy of it. It's choosing to release ourselves from the bondage that the offense has placed on our lives. Administering grace is choosing to withhold judgment when we want to ridicule, criticize or condemn. It is understanding that although others may have missed the mark, fallen or experienced a public failure, and even though we may have just cause to render judgment against them, we choose to bestow undeserved, unmerited favor instead. This is the workings of grace. In reality we may have personal knowledge of someone else's failures, sin, or even worse, we may have been victimized, betrayed or wronged by them. We call this having stones. Yet, it does not give us the right to continually exploit their weakness or failures for our advantage, so that we can continuously exact revenge on them. Whenever we desire revenge, or to bring or return harm to others, we are of the wrong spirit. I specifically can recall an incident when I was offended by something spoken to me to intentionally hurt me. Their words offended and cut me to my core. I could sense their satisfaction in what they had accomplished. In purposeful retaliation I thought of the most hurtful, yet true words that I could speak to them in return to cause them to hurt as they had hurt me. Immediately, I responded in my flesh and I released a verbal assault in return upon the individual. My words were purposefully mean spirited and intentionally hurtful. I had accomplished my goal. I immediately sensed their pain and simultaneously I experienced the conviction of the Holy Spirit chastising me, because as a believer I was out of order. God was not pleased with my response. At that very moment I realized I needed to drop my stones and Get My Mind Right!

Luke 9:25 KJV "But he turned, and rebuked them, and said, Ye know not what manner of spirit ye are of."

Whenever we find pleasure in someone else's pain or misfortune, we are acting opposite of the character and integrity of Christ. Throughout scripture we are continually admonished to bless and not curse those who mistreat us. Christ is trying to teach us about His love which is demonstrated through grace and mercy. Afterall, we ALL live in glass houses whether we realize it or not. We have all sinned. Sin is sin to God. My sin is not smaller than yours. Life can be extremely fragile at times. We do not need anyone attacking, belittling or trying to cause us problems or trying to destroy our lives just as this is something that we all should strive not to do to others. In all honesty, at times, life within itself can be very challenging and overwhelming. Life is really hard sometimes. How many times have you been experiencing a private and personal challenge that you had not chosen to share with others, well at any given moment others are also experiencing challenges and difficulties that you know nothing about. This is why it is so important that we do not throw stones. We should instead choose to show mercy, or simply, leave people alone. It is unbecoming for a believer to be a hell raiser by sowing discord instead of love, being judgmental and critical instead of merciful and kind. If it was not for the goodness of the Lord, where would we be. We have all felt disappointments, been offended and hurt, just as if we would simply be honest we would have to acknowledge that at one time or another, that we too have hurt, offended and disappointed others, even if it was unintentional. Each of us desire to be given a second chance, but in most instances, we struggle with releasing others, so that they can begin anew and have another opportunity also. The bible clearly states that we will be judged using the same measurement that we use to judge others with. I am not suggesting condoning ungodly behavior. I am encouraging you to always show compassion instead of being judgmental. I am suggesting you extend grace instead of a critical spirit. Extending mercy and grace toward others always results in the reaping of the same. It may not be from the same person whom you extended it to, but guaranteed it returns to you more abundantly. In scripture when the woman was caught in adultery, Jesus being the only righteous one and being able to judge, chose instead to show love and mercy, this is a very powerful story:

John 8:10-11 KJV "When Jesus had lifted up himself, and saw none but the woman, he said unto the, Woman, where are those times thine accusers? Hath

no man condemned thee? She said, No man, Lord and Jesus said unto her, Neither do I condemn thee: go, and sin no more."

Dropping the stones is about much more than just forgiving others, it is about 'choosing to do no harm'. When we have been harmed by others, or experienced severe pain it sometimes changes our emotional makeup. Being hurt or wounded can make you very defensive and sometimes we can even take on the characteristics of the ones that hurt us and we in turn become victimizers. Think back on your situation, think about how it feels when others judge or condemn you. Have you ever been in a difficult place, going through your day trying your best to keep it together and have someone out of the blue to be kind to you or give you a compliment. That individual may not have any idea how positively they impacted your day, but you do. They had no way of knowing that you were in a bad place. Each day we need to start considering that possibly the individuals that we come in contact with on a daily basis may be in a hidden or private crisis that we know nothing about and our interactions with them can have a significant positive impact on their outlook on not just that day, but on their life. By choosing to drop the stones, it will free you up to walk in a greater abundance of joy and happiness in your own life. The energy that was required for you to walk in and maintain a spirit of unforgiveness toward others once released will now be readily available for you to utilize in managing and enjoying your own life.

Luke 6:31-35 KJV *"And as ye would that men should do to you, do ye also to them likewise. For if ye love them which love you, what thank have ye? for sinners also love those that love them. And if ye do good to them which do good to you, what thank have ye? for sinners also do even the same. And if ye lend to them* *of whom ye hope to receive, what thank have ye? for sinners also lend to sinners, to receive as much again. But love ye your enemies, and do good, and lend, hoping for nothing again; and your reward shall be great, and ye shall be the children of the Highest: for he is kind unto the unthankful and to the evil."*

9   I CAN DO IT!

***Philippians 4:13 AMPC** "I have strength for all things in Christ Who empowers me [I am ready for anything and equal to anything through Him Who [a]infuses inner strength into me; I am [b]self-sufficient in Christ's sufficiency]."*

Walking in the revelation that I can handle whatever comes my way has been freeing for me. I don't think I ever truly understood how fearful and afraid I was walking through life, until I became free from feeling like I was constantly on the verge of failure and breakdown. Whenever we survive a major difficulty, knowing that it was no way possible that we did it through our own strength or ability, but by depending solely on God. It creates in us what I call a 'I Can Do It' mentality. I believe that this is the will of God for every believer, not that we experience major life obstacles, but that we understand that in the midst of our darkest and most challenging times in life, that God will never leave or forsake us. He is there for us continually, showing himself to be our strength. On the other side of I can not, is a I can. I often think of Satan, as being a bully, a toothless lion that roams about seeking whom he can destroy. The scripture states that he goes about seeking for someone He can steal from, kill and destroy.

***1 Peter 5:8 AMPC** "Be well balanced (temperate, sober of mind), be vigilant and cautious at all times; for that enemy of yours, the devil, roams*

***around like a lion roaring [[a]in fierce hunger], seeking someone to* seize upon *and* devour".**

I believe that this someone is the individual who does not know their identity in Christ. He is actively seeking his next victim, and because we hear this so often, I believe that sometimes it sets us up to believe that he is the powerful predator and we are weaklings mercifully in his hands. I think that somehow, we have misrepresented this picture in our minds. Although Satan is on the prowl, he is more like a toothless lion whose main power is in his ability to deceive the believer into believing that he is fiercer than he actually is. Satan's mere appearance in the believer's life most times is all that is needed to make us take on a defensive instead of an offensive stance. It should not be this way. You are powerful, and you have the ability to walk in victory.

I John 4:4 NIV "You, dear children, are from God and have overcome them, because the one who is in you is greater than the one who is in the world."

As believers we must constantly remind ourselves and each other that despair and defeat is not the will of God concerning us. Bad things do happen to good people. However, God did not cause any calamity that we have experienced in our lives. Only good and perfect gifts come from the Father. God set up a system of operation for our lives here on earth. He stated that he gave us the authority and power to govern the earth, therefore it is no longer under his control but ours. I do not believe that God is in heaven flipping coins regarding my life. Heads I win, tails I lose. No, I believe that regardless of what we encounter in life that we yet have the choice to remain in faith and respond in a godly way. I do not have all the answers but I know that God is faithful and if I trust him, all things will work out for my good.

Unexpected things are going to happen. We are going to experience tribulation in this life. Christ forewarned us of this, so that we would not be caught off guard when we are faced with difficulties in life.

John 16:33 AMPC *"I have told you these things, so that in Me you may have [perfect] peace and confidence. In the world you have tribulation and trials and distress and frustration; but be of good cheer [take courage; be confident, certain, undaunted]! For I have overcome the world. [I have deprived it of power to harm you and have conquered it for you.]"*

We know that we will encounter difficult seasons in life, and we also know according to the Word of God that we are instructed to be of good courage in the midst of these seasons. This is only possible when we take the 'I Can' attitude. It is not that we welcome a trial or obstacle when we see it coming, but it is that we don't become cowardly and run away from it either. Knowing that 'I can' gives me the wherewithal to face whatever comes my way with the attitude and conviction that I can do all things through Christ who strengthens me, including face, survive and thrive in the midst of the trial I am experiencing.

Proverbs 29:11 AMPC *" For I know the plans I have for you," declares the LORD, "plans to prosper you and not to harm you, plans to give you hope and a future.*

Problems cannot be avoided in life. It rains on the just as well as the unjust. Children of God we possess something that the unjust do not have and that is an assurance from God that we can conquer any obstacle. We can handle whatever comes our way, if we believe that we can handle it. Most of us are familiar with the story of the little engine that could. Victory over every obstacle always begins in our mind. When we are first faced with life's challenges, our mindset, the way we view the situation, event or circumstance is pivotal. At that very moment, we have to begin to decree out of our own mouths, into the atmosphere, even if we don't believe it at the time, that 'I think I can, I think I can'. We must believe and know according to scripture, that faith is established as we continually and consistently hear the Word of God. There is not a more powerful method of hearing, than when we are individually hearing the Word of God that we have received being echoed from the depths of our being. Faith is voice activated, that is why it is important that we voice what the Word of God says concerning us, into our own personal lives. Hearing others speak the Word to us and listening to the Word being preached does not exempt us from having to speak the Word out of our mouths into our situations. What are you daily saying about your life? You need to hear yourself speaking God's Word into your own life.

Romans 10:17 AMPC "So faith comes by hearing [what is told], and what is heard comes by the preaching [of the message that came from the lips] of Christ (the Messiah Himself)"

Just as the little engine began to exclaim 'I think I Can' when it appeared to be an uphill battle that was more powerful than his little caboose could handle, he yet stated I think I can. During your situation, right where you are, you must begin to decree out loud into the atmosphere, I Can!. You need to hear yourself proclaim your expectations in advance before they manifest. Don't allow your situation to intimidate you into being silent. Refuse to believe that you can not accomplish the task. Do not allow what you are facing to make you feel unsettled in any way. Don't allow your situation to convince you that you have to handle it within your own strength or abilities.

***Romans 8:37 AMP** "Yet in all these things we are more than conquerors and gain an overwhelming victory through Him who loved us {so much that He died for us}."*

I have found it easier to agree with the devil upfront and admit that I cannot handle life on my own. Within myself I realize that I am totally out matched, but with Christ I know that I am more than able to walk in victory. Christ has already won the victory for me. Yes, in Christ I got this. In Christ I Win. It does not matter what it looks like or feels like, with Christ I know that I Can. With Christ YOU CAN too!

***1 Corinthians 15:57-58** "But thanks be to God, Who gives us the victory [making us conquerors] through our Lord Jesus Christ. Therefore, my beloved brethren, be firm (steadfast), immovable, always abounding in the work of the Lord [always being superior, excelling, doing more than enough in the service of the Lord], knowing and being continually aware that your labor in the Lord is not futile [it is never wasted or to no purpose].*

10 LIVING FROM THE INSIDE OUT!

Isaiah 26:3 AMPC "You will guard him and keep him in perfect and constant peace whose mind [both its inclination and its character] is stayed on You, because he commits himself to You, leans on You, and hopes confidently in You"

I have spent most of my life up to this point believing and acting as though the key to possessing and maintaining true inner peace was dependent on what was going on around me or happening in my life at the time. To me, this made sense. How could you expect someone who was in the midst of a chaotic situation in their personal life or environment to maintain their inner peace? In the past, I didn't realize what I have now come to understand and believe. I now know from personal experience, that it is possible to have and maintain inner peace in the midst of your most difficult and challenging season. You can experience peace, even when you have been thrust into the unexpected and the unimaginable. However, the only way that this peace can be accessed, is by your willingness and obedience to hear, believe and trust in the Word of God. You must be willing to keep your mind stayed on the Word of God both day and night. This is not an easy task. By nature, we tend to meditate on and become fixated on the problems at hand. At times you may feel like the more you focus on the problem, the quicker it will be resolved. This is because we feel we have to take care of our problems ourselves. However, this is so opposite of the truth. The more we focus on the problem, the bigger the problem becomes in our minds. I am not suggesting denying what is going on in your life. I am simply stating that the only way to walk in the peace of God in the midst of trials and tribulation is to give more priority to what the Word says than you are giving to your problems.

Philippians 4:6-7 AMP "Do not be anxious or worried about anything, but in everything [every circumstance and situation] by prayer and petition with thanksgiving, continue to make your [specific] requests known to God. And the peace of God [that peace which reassures the heart, that peace] which transcends all understanding, [that peace which] stands guard over your hearts and your minds in Christ Jesus [is yours]"

The size of the situation, circumstance or event may vary; however, the solution or answer remains the same. Are you willing to spend time meditating on the Word of God, day and night so that the Word can replace the doubt, worry and anxiety that you are experiencing? Receiving and possessing the peace of God comes as a result of hearing and meditating on the Word of God. Peace is a part of the believer's covenant. Unexplainable peace is connected to our obedience and willingness to keep our minds stayed on Him. He assumes the responsibility of keeping our minds in perfect peace. Therefore, it does not matter what is happening externally in our lives. None of that matters to God or decreases his desire or ability to keep us in peace. It is not your peace that we are trying to access, it is the peace that belongs to and comes from Him.

John 14:27 KJV "Peace I leave with you, my peace I give unto you: not as the world giveth, give I unto

you. Let not your heart be troubled, neither let it be afraid."

Living inside out is allowing the inner peace of the Holy Spirit, which you recieve from keeping your mind stayed on the Word of God, to permeate from inside you outward into all the various areas of your life. Do not allow what is happening in your marriage, finances, health or relationships to determine whether or not you will be at peace. We will never be able to completely control what happens around us, and that realization alone can be the source of great anxiety. However, knowing that keeping your mind on the Word of God will bring you unexplainable peace should be a source of greater comfort.

Philippians 4:7 KJV "And the peace of God, which passeth all understanding, shall keep your hearts and minds through Christ Jesus."

Inner peace is a gift from the Father to the believer. It is a gift that can only be unwrapped through our faith in God's Word. Having love one for another and possessing the peace of God are two things that identify that we are his children and that we are not of this world. It is vitally important that during our most difficult times that we allow God to use us, to show himself strong through us, to the world. There is nothing special or unusual about being happy and at peace when everything is going well in your life. The ungodly even rejoice when things are well. The litmus test of our faith in God is our ability to rejoice and remain at peace when everything seems to be going wrong and appears opposite of what we are believing for it to be. Living inside out, is having confidence that what you possess within you, can and will sustain you, through whatever situation, circumstance or event that you may encounter.

2 Corinthians 4:7 KJV "But we have this treasure in earthen vessels, that the excellency of the power may be of God, and not of us"

Living inside out is understanding that you have been given and now possess a powerful, life changing treasure within yourself. This treasure is the Holy Spirit which came to dwell within you when you accepted Christ as Lord and Savior. His presence is a game changer. He strengthens, teaches and comforts the believer so that we are more than able to handle whatever life challenges we encounter. God's presence in our lives is a stabilizing force. He will never leave or forsake us. We are not alone. We can do all things through Christ which strengthens us. We are more than conquerors. Do not allow what is happening externally in your life to determine or establish your level of inner peace. Allow the peace of God within you to permeate outwardly to the various areas of your life and relationships. Living from the inside out is daily facing life with this assurances that the Holy Spirit will direct us through life daily by his spirit which dwells on the inside of us.

11   YOU HAVE TO LOVE YOU!

Psalms 139:14 KJV "I will praise thee; for I am fearfully and wonderfully made: marvellous are thy works; and that my soul knoweth right well."

Learning to truly love myself is a journey that I am yet on. All of my life I have been very critical of myself, especially of my body. I have never really been totally satisfied with or accepting of my physical appearance. On a daily basis I have found myself not being able to look in the mirror at myself, without struggling to not nitpick myself. In the past, the object of my displeasure targeted my height, weight, birthmarks, feet or the way I looked in general. In times past, I have often discovered that unintentionally, I have been my own worst critic or enemy. I am sure I am not the only one that has been guilty of this behavior. Attacking, criticizing, complaining about and sometimes even hating the way we look is not the will of God for us. Many of you are identifying with me right now by automatically thinking about the things about your own bodies that you dislike or hate. Attacking oneself emotionally is a great example of NOT having your mind right. Tearing yourself down, belittling or berating your appearance, along with negative self-talk, all fall under the guidelines of self-hatred which is the opposite of love. If you are struggling to love yourself, it is ridiculous to expect anyone else to be able to give to you, what you have been unwilling or unable to do for yourself. Satan gives us negative thoughts, ideas and suggestions about our bodies in order to influence our perception of ourselves. His goal is to decrease our overall self-esteem. He attacks our self-image, because he wants us to believe the lie. Satan does not want us feeling good about ourselves. He especially does not want us to love or value ourselves. He wants us to think negatively about ourselves within and echo those thoughts out loud when we speak. He understands the power of self-love. He understands that our thoughts about ourselves influence how we feel about ourselves. What we think on a daily basis about ourselves will govern what we will allow to continue to exist and remain in our lives and how we will react or respond to life's situations.

Proverbs 23:7a KJV "As he thinketh in his heart, so is he:"

In essence, Satan knows that the things we allow and permit in our lives are based on what we think and feel about ourselves inwardly. Outwardly, we may put on the facade that we think that we are all that. Our faces may be made up or 'beat' with eyebrows on fleak. We may have every hair in place, manicure, pedicure and may be dressed to impress. We can look beautiful on the outside, while at the same time inwardly, we are consumed with feelings of inadequacy and self-loathing. The way that others have talked to us or treated us may have left us feeling like we are not quite good enough. Inwardly, we may be struggling with low self-esteem. The truth is that we are not fooling anyone. The way that we treat ourselves and the way we allow others to treat us is an indication of both how much we truly love ourselves and also the degree to which we value ourselves. People who love themselves won't allow themselves to be continually abused in any way. They understand that they deserve better. They have non-negotiables in place regarding how they will be treated, and one of the most important ones is that they will not allow abusive behavior to continue to exist toward or around them. They understand that they are better than that. They will not allow abuse to remain unchallenged in their lives. If you are allowing continued abuse in your life of any kind, whether emotional, verbal or physical, you need to get your mind right! You deserve better! You are valuable to God! It does not matter what you have been through or what you are currently going through. It doesn't matter what you feel you permitted to happen in the past, you can decide today that you will no longer tolerate disrespect or abuse of any kind to continue in your life. You are loved by God.

Romans 12:1 KJV "I beseech you therefore, brethren, by the mercies of God, that ye present your bodies a living sacrifice, holy, acceptable unto God, which is your reasonable service."

We are to present our bodies to God as living sacrifices, holy and acceptable unto Him which is our reasonable service. Yes, HE wants your body and we are to present it to him. We are to give God our bodies as a present. He wants our bodies because our body houses and transports our spirit within the earth realm. In order for you to be legal in the earth, your spirit which is eternal has to occupy and utilize a body. That is why Satan attacks our perception of our bodies, as well as our physical health. We become his ally when we don't love and care for ourselves properly. We can not afford to allow abuse to remain unchecked in our lives. You were born into the earth to fulfill a predestined purpose. No one can do what God specifically created you to do, like you can do it. Perhaps, you don't know what your purpose is. Most likely not being aware of what your purpose is can be traced back to you not having your mind right. Lack of self-love is a ploy of the enemy to cause you to feel inadequate which hinders you from realizing your purpose and ultimately robs you of living an abundant, satisfied and long life.

Ephesians 2:10 KJV "For we are his workmanship, created in Christ Jesus unto good works, which God hath before ordained that we should walk in them."

You are lovable and worthy of love. Do not internalize the way you have been treated as being a reflection of your self-worth. The hurt and abuse you may have suffered did not happen to you because of your lack of worth. The devil is a liar and the truth is NOT in him. Our abusers are individuals who did not understand their purpose and worth. Abuse is never about the victim, it is always about the abuser. It is important for you to truly know that the way someone treats you whether it is good or bad, is not a reflection of who you are, but it is a direct reflection of who they are. For too long we have measured our self-worth by how others treat us. This is not a fair assessment, instead we need to see ourselves through the eyes of our creator. We must stop seeing ourselves through the eyes of flawed men. Jesus loved you so much that he thought you were worth dying for. As a teenager I struggled with low self-esteem. Basically, I guess, looking back over my life I can now recognize that I have questioned my own self-worth most of my life. Shortly after I became a Christian I remember talking to my pastor Brother Bobby Tidwell, an amazing man of God about struggling to truly accept and love myself. He told me that I was special and valuable to the Father, and that He sent Jesus specifically to die for me, so that He could demonstrate His love for me. I replied, no he didn't die just for me, he died for the world, good people. I just happen to be the beneficiary of what Jesus did. His reply permanently changed how I thought about Christ's death on the cross. He replied no, when Jesus died, he had you on his mind. He died specifically for you. Wow, I couldn't fathom that at the time, but now I am convinced of the Father's love specifically for me. His love for me has empowered me to see myself as lovable and valuable. It has convinced me to care for myself. I now know that if I was the only person in the entire world, my Father would have yet sent Jesus to rescue me. He saw me as worth it and as a result of that revelation of the Father's love for me, I can boldly proclaim that I have learned to accept and love myself conditionally. You too must learn to love yourself because you are valuable to God. You are enough!

John 3:16 KJV *"For God so loved the world, that he gave his only begotten Son, that whosoever believeth in him should not perish, but have everlasting life."*

12   Reclaiming My Time!

Isaiah 61:7 KJV "For your shame ye shall have double; and for confusion they shall rejoice in their portion: therefore, in their land they shall possess the double: everlasting joy shall be unto them."

It is natural for an individual who has gone through a life altering event, circumstance or situation, that was devastating in nature, and beyond their control, to realize afterwards that they may yet experience and battle a profound sense of personal loss or self-identity. In reality they may find that they have been forever changed. They may no longer recognize the individual that they have become. The time invested or spent focused on or dealing with their situation most likely has also resulted in them feeling like they have wasted or lost a lot of time. They may even feel like they have been robbed. However, this does not have to be or remain your truth. The change in who you are does not have to be all entirely bad. With the right mindset, it is possible for you to become a better version of yourself and for you to reclaim your time I personally know that one of the most awesome things about having an intimate relationship with the Father is that if you will allow him to, he will take the broken pieces of your life and turn them into both a lesson and a blessing for both you and others. There are no limitations or deficits in Christ. Our success is not determined by the precipitating events in our lives. Our destiny is determined by our willingness and obedience to learn whatever lesson we can from our past experiences along with our commitment to letting go of all past hurts, disappointments, and unforgiveness. We let go for our own benefit, so that we will no longer be held hostage to the past. Our success is solely dependent on our determination and resilience to move forward. In essence, it is dependent on our commitment to getting and keeping our minds right which is a daily decision. God desires to fix it. Honestly speaking, even though you would have never chosen or volunteered to go through what you have been through in a million years. If you will allow God to use IT, he will take it, and cause it to work out for your good and His glory. It will most definitely be undeniably easy for you and others to see and identify the blessings you have experienced as a result of your challenging situation. You will have gained more than you have lost. As a result of getting our minds right, we have been positioned to reap the unforeseen benefits of grace, wisdom, strength and dependency on the Father, which was gained as a result of what we have been through.

Romans 8:28 KJV "And we know that all things work together for good to them that love God, to them who are the called according to his purpose"

God is faithful! He will give you beauty for your ashes. But, you must be willing and ready to make the exchange. You can NOT receive beauty if you refuse to give up and release your ashes. Ashes are all that you are left with when ALL has been destroyed by fire.

Isaiah 61:3 KJV "To appoint unto them that mourn in Zion, to give unto them beauty for ashes, the oil of joy for mourning, the garment of praise for the spirit of heaviness; that they might be called trees of righteousness, the planting of the Lord, that he might be glorified"

With the right perspective, each day will be the beginning of a new season in your life. You must be willing to let it be a new day. Each new day brings with it new opportunities and possibilities. It is time for you to reclaim your time. Please don't waste any more energy whining and complaining about the circumstances, situations and events that you have had to face or are currently having to face in life. I am truly sorry. If I could fix it for you, I would. If I could have rewinded my own life, I would have done it. But, that is not how it works. You have to accept and be willing to move forward with the life that you now possess. Get Your Mind Right! Start anew on today. Face whatever you have to deal with head on. Burying your head in the sand will not make the past go away. Ignoring it does not change it either. It will remain the same until you decide within your very being, that you will no longer allow the past to define who you are and impact the remainder of your life. I can't stop or change all the circumstances, situations and events that I have had to experience in my life. However, I am responsible for how I respond to them. Complaining does not change anything. It is literally a waste of your precious time and energy. If you are alive and able to read this book, then there is hope for you. You can move forward. Throughout this book you have been reading about the way we think and about having the right mindset. Well, this is where the rubber meets the road. It is totally up to you what you are going to do with what you have received. It is completely your decision. No one can decide for you. No one can live your life for you. Your life journey is individually and uniquely your own. You have to make up your own mind that you are determined to move forward by refusing to become or remain stagnant. You now have the tools to Keep it Moving!

Philippians 3:14 KJV "I press toward the mark for the prize of the high calling of God in Christ Jesus"

Yes, forward movement begins with the right mindset. You have to make a conscious decision to progress onward in the direction of *Life.* Prayerfully, your thinking is in a better place by now, and you too are in the process of allowing God to get your mind right. I hope you are seeing things much clearer than you ever have before. Get Your Mind Right should be as if you have been given a new pair of glasses that allow you to see things now, that you were unaware that were there all along. Things around us do not have to necessarily change for us to change, because it is the realization and acceptance of this, that will allow us to get rid of that kind of faulty thinking and be willing to embrace truth. Thinking as a victim is weighty and it holds us back from not only moving forward but also from taking ownership of the present condition of our lives. I want to be one of the many witnesses that are surrounding you and telling you to let it go, to cast aside incorrect thinking and *Get Your Mind Right!*

Hebrews 12:1 KJV "Wherefore seeing we also are compassed about with so great a cloud of witnesses, let us lay aside every weight, and the sin which doth so easily beset us, and let us run with patience the race that is set before us."

I am excited about the future which lies before you. I am so thankful for being able to share Get Your Mind Right with you. As a result of being able to share the biblical principles I've learned with you through this book, it is my prayer that you feel more empowered now than ever before. I pray that when you encounter situations, events or circumstances that are beyond your control and are not of your own making, that you will never allow yourself to feel that you are ever a helpless victim again. I pray that you feel empowered because you understand that you have the power to choose the direction of your life which begins with you having your mind right. You can always choose life and to walk in victory.

Deuteronomy 30:19 AMP *"I call heaven and earth as witnesses against you today, that I have set before you life and death, the blessing and the curse; therefore, you shall choose life in order that you may live, you and your descendants"*

Anytime that we feel that choice has been taken away from us, we feel less in control of everything. I am encouraged about moving forward because I know that my ability to decide and choose for myself is intact. As a matter of fact, I am wiser and stronger than I have ever been. I possess a zeal within myself that is pushing me to believe God for more and to step out on faith more. I am determined to reclaim my time. This book is the direct result of my having gone through the most difficult and unimaginable season of my life. It was in the midst of my personal trial that I heard the Holy Spirit within me instructing me to 'Get My Mind Right'. The beautiful result of that devastating time in my life is that this book was birthed. God took the pain, shame, and disappointment that I was experiencing, and turned it into not just a book, but a movement. Look at God! Won't he do It?

Joel 2:25 KJV "And I will restore to you the years that the locust hath eaten, the cankerworm, and the caterpillar, and the palmerworm, my great army which I sent among you"

If you are afraid of the future and of moving forward that is an indicator that your mind is still not completely right. Life is simply our spirit's journey while in the earth realm. While on this journey we will sometimes experience delays, detours and sometimes we will even get lost. We make wrong turns and sometimes we will even fall into the ditch or run off the cliff. However, if we are yet living, then there is yet a way out to the other side. Our earth journey is unique to each one of us. No two journeys are exactly the same, they are like our fingerprints. God has individualized them perfectly for each one of us. That is why no one can live your life for you or get your mind right for you. Your life is in your own hands. Listen to me, when we get lost, make mistakes or mess up, we can't just stop moving forward. We cannot just become stagnant and remain in that same lost posture forever.

"If you can't fly then run, if you can't run then walk, if you can't walk then crawl, but whatever you do you have to keep moving forward. "Martin Luther King Jr.

Anything living that does not move will soon lose hope, weaken and die. We must recalculate or regroup and continue on with the remainder of our journey. A Right Mind is all that you need in order to see that your situation is not hopeless.

2 Corinthians 4:17 "For our light, momentary affliction (this slight distress of the passing hour) is ever more and more abundantly preparing and producing and achieving for us an everlasting weight of glory [beyond all measure, excessively surpassing all comparisons and all calculations, a vast and transcendent glory and blessedness never to cease!],"

A right mind sees options and possibilities beyond the natural, visible realm. A right mind gives you hope for the future because through faith you are assured that God will restore to you all that you have lost or had stolen from you. Allow God to show you a glimpse of your future so that you can obtain a vision of what your life can yet be. Vision of your future is absolutely necessary for you to both Reclaim Your Time and Get and Keep Your Mind Right. Blessings!!!

Proverbs 29:18 KJV "Where there is no vision, the people perish: but he that keepeth the law, happy is he."

ABOUT THE AUTHOR

Angela J. Walker is a motivational speaker, life coach, teacher, and author. Angela's passion is to be a catalyst to encourage and inspire believers to renew their minds and get them right according to the Word of God and to live empowered, transformed lives. Angela has experienced several unimaginable events in her life that had the potential to destroy her but instead she chose to use them to propel her into intentionally walking into her purpose. She has been in ministry for over 30 years. She currently leads the women's ministry of her church which she co-founded with her husband on January 2, 2000. She has been married for 32 years and has three wonderful adult children and one grandchild.

CONTACT INFORMATION FOR SPEAKING ENGAGEMENT

Angela J. Walker
c/o Deliverance Family Worship Center
406 Scott Street
Jonesboro, AR 72401
(870) 931-5453
angela.walker@dfwc.org
getyourmindright247@gmail.com

Made in the USA
Middletown, DE
09 November 2021